THE HORROR OF THE HOLOCAUST

by Claire Throp

Consultant: Philip Parker
Author and historian

capstone

Infosearch books are published by Capstone Press,
1710 Roe Crest Drive, North Mankato, Minnesota 56003
www.mycapstone.com

Library of Congress Cataloging-in-Publication Data
Library of Congress Cataloging-in-Publication data is available on the Library of Congress website.

978-1-4846-4166-8 (library binding)
978-1-4846-4170-5 (paperback)
978-1-4846-4174-3 (eBook PDF)

Editorial Credits
Editor: Claire Throp
Designer: Clare Nicholas
Production Specialist: Kathy McColley
Media Researchers: Claire Throp,
Steve White-Thomson and Izzi Howell
Illustrators: Ron Dixon and Clare Nicholas

Photo Credits
Alamy: dpa picture alliance archive, 34, 37, Everett Collection Historical, 20 (b), 28, 41, Granger Historical Picture Archive, 38, Image Bank, 13, INTERFOTO, 7, United Archives GmbH, 35, World History Archive, 10, 26, 33; iStock: martin-dm, 4, RonaldWJansen, 39, slowcentury, 17; Mary Evans: Sueddeutsche Zeitung Photo, 30; Shutterstock: Aksenenko Olga, 3, 44 -45 (dirt), caminoel, 29, Daniel DeSlover, 43, Elzbieta Sekowska, 9 (t), ESB Professional, 22, Everett Historical, 1, 6, 8, 11, 12, 15, 16, 19 (b), 23, 27, katatonia82, 31, kavalenkava, 5, Martial Red, 5 (skull and crossbones), 32, 39 (skull), monbibi, 35 (old book), Naci Yavuz, 9 (b), Nuttapong, 3, 44 -45 (barbed wire), Pavel Huspeka, 20 (t), pisaphotography, 42, REAL TIME IT02794870960, 24, Robert Hoetink, 36 (m), 36 (r), Rolf E. Staerk, 25, Santi Rodriguez, 36 (l); Superstock: World History Archive/World History Archive, cover; Wikimedia: Bundesarchiv, Bild 183-R99621/CC-BY-SA 3.0, 19 (t), Fundacion Memoria del Holocausto, Argentina, 21.

Printed in the United States 5657

Table of Contents

What Was the Holocaust?

Between 1933 and 1945, nearly 6 million **Jewish people** were killed. Millions of others, including Romani people (also called gypsies), as well as disabled and gay people, were killed. People who did not agree with those who were in charge were killed. This mass murder is known as the Holocaust. It was carried out by Adolf Hitler and his **political party**, the Nazis.

Hitler and the Nazis wanted Germany to be one **Aryan** race, which they considered better than anyone else. People were forced into **ghettos**, **concentration camps**, and later **death camps**. Auschwitz played an important role in the Nazis' plans for Jewish people during the war. It was a concentration camp and death camp. Prisoners were mainly killed in **gas chambers**.

Auschwitz was the main killing center for the Nazis during the war.

The word *Holocaust* comes from the Greek language. It means sacrifice by fire. It has come to mean the great destruction of large numbers of people. Jewish people use the word *Shoah* to describe the horrific events carried out by the government of Nazi Germany. It means ruin or waste.

HISTORY UNLOCKED

We often use primary sources to learn about the past. A primary source is a document, photograph, or artifact made during the time that is being studied. Letters, diaries, and speeches are all primary sources.

Tourists visit the house where Anne Frank hid in Amsterdam, the Netherlands. **See pages 34–35 for Anne's story.**

Who Were the Nazis?

Adolf Hitler was born in April 1889 in Austria. He moved to Germany in 1913. When World War I began in 1914, Hitler fought for his new country. When Germany surrendered in 1918, Hitler was angry. Even though there was no proof, he believed that Jewish people were to blame.

Hitler already hated Jewish people. After the war, he joined the German Workers' Party. They also hated Jewish people. In 1920, the party stated that once in power they would make sure that Jewish people had fewer **rights** than other Germans. They would limit the ability of Jewish people to go to university, for example.

This poster says, "The war is his fault!" The man shown is Jewish – he is wearing a yellow star.

THE NAZI PARTY

Hitler was very good at giving speeches. The leaders of the party were worried about how popular he was. Soon, Hitler became the party's leader. It was renamed the National Socialist German Workers' Party. It became better known as the Nazi Party. From 1930, the party became more and more popular.

A NEW CHANCELLOR

In January 1933, Hitler became Chancellor, or leader, of Germany. He quickly worked to get rid of anyone who was against him. Such people were often imprisoned in concentration camps such as Dachau, which opened in March 1933.

From 1933 to 1939, more than 400 new rules against Jewish people were brought out. In April 1933, a limit was placed on the number of Jewish people allowed to go to school or university. On April 1, 1933, Hitler called for Germans to boycott Jewish shops and businesses. Former soldiers called **Storm Troopers** stood outside shops with signs. These said "Don't buy from Jews."

These signs read "Germans Defend Yourselves! Do not buy from Jews!"

THE JEWISH PEOPLE

In ancient times, the Jewish people had lived in the kingdoms of Judah and Israel (an area later called Palestine). But by the end of the 1st century, millions of Jewish people had settled in different countries. Most of the time, they lived peacefully.

Sometimes, though, Jewish people were badly treated. They had been forced out of England in 1290. They had been forced out of France in 1394. They had been murdered in Poland and Ukraine in 1648. But they had lived with some freedom in Germany in the 1920s.

ANTI-SEMITISM

Hatred of Jewish people for no clear reason is known as **anti-Semitism**. Nazis blamed Jewish people for many of Germany's problems. They even blamed Jewish people for Germany losing World War I, even though Jewish Germans fought alongside them. Non-Jewish Germans were made to believe that Jewish people had cheated them.

Germany lost World War I. But the families of German soldiers welcomed them home.

HISTORY UNLOCKED

In 1922, a writer named Josef Hell asked Hitler what he would do if he came to power.

"If I am ever really in power, the destruction of the Jews will be my first and most important job."

The Nazis wanted Germany to contain only a certain type of people. They were white people born in northern Europe. They had blonde hair, blue eyes, and were tall. Hitler called them Aryans. He believed that they were better than anyone else.

From 1941, Jewish people were forced to wear a yellow star on their clothes. The star stood for the Star of David, a Jewish religious symbol. The stars were to show everyone that the people wearing them were Jewish. A star was also placed in Jewish shop windows. A "J" was stamped in Jewish passports.

The stars Jewish people had to wear were made of a very bright yellow, rough material. *Jude* means Jew in German.

NUREMBERG LAWS

In September 1935, the Nuremberg Laws reduced the freedom of Jewish people even more. If a person had at least three Jewish grandparents, they were considered Jewish. This was even if they no longer believed in the Jewish religion. Jewish people were no longer German **citizens**. This meant they had fewer rights. They were not allowed to marry anyone who was not also Jewish. The laws made it clear that Jewish people were not welcome in Germany.

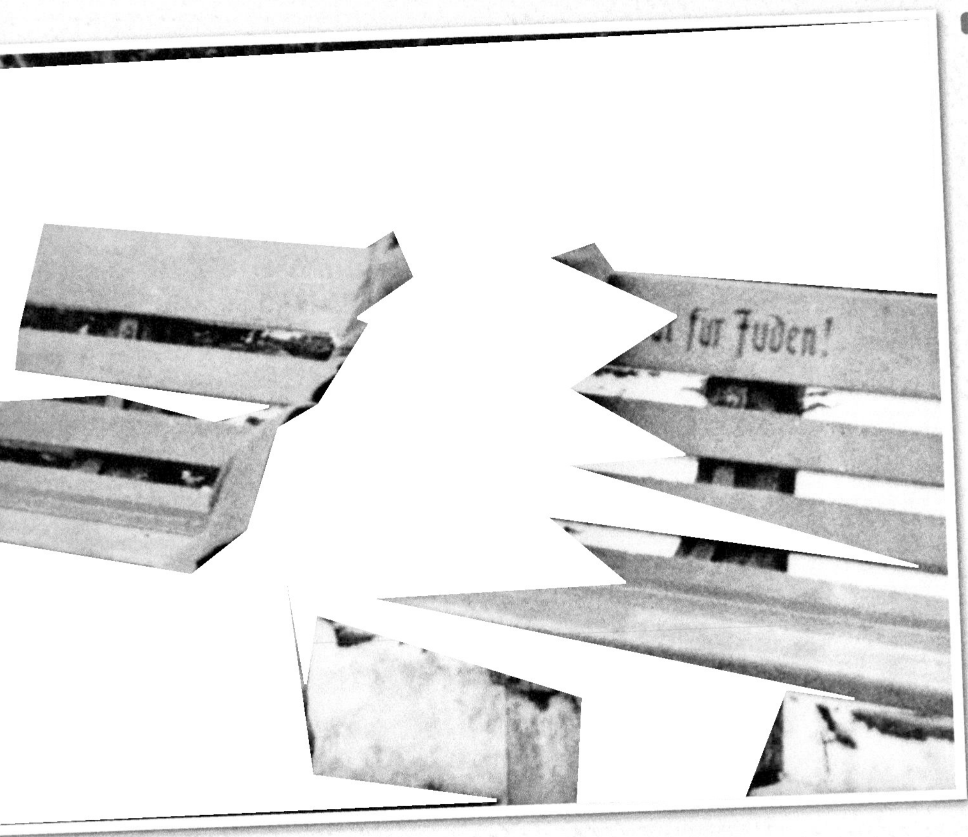

This woman is sitting on a bench marked "Only for Jews" in Austria. The Nazis wanted to keep Jewish people separate from non-Jewish people.

After the Nuremberg Laws, more anti-Jewish rules and laws were put in place. Some of these were national, but others were local. For example, Jewish patients were no longer allowed to go to hospitals in Düsseldorf, Germany. In December 1935, Jewish soldiers were no longer allowed to be named among the dead on World War I memorials.

The Nazis were making it impossible for Jewish people to earn a living in Germany. Jewish people had to tell the government about everything they owned. Jewish businesses were taken over by non-Jewish Germans. They were able to buy the businesses for very little money. By April 1938, the number of Jewish-owned businesses in Germany had fallen by about two-thirds.

"UNFIT" PEOPLE

It wasn't only Jewish people who were suffering. Between 1933 and 1939, 360,000 people were forced into having operations. The operations meant that they would be unable to bear children. These were people that the Nazis thought were "unfit." They included disabled people and those who were deaf or blind.

The Nazis liked to hold large gatherings called rallies to keep Nazi supporters excited about the party. This one took place at Nuremberg in September 1933. Rallies were also used to show other countries how powerful the Nazis were.

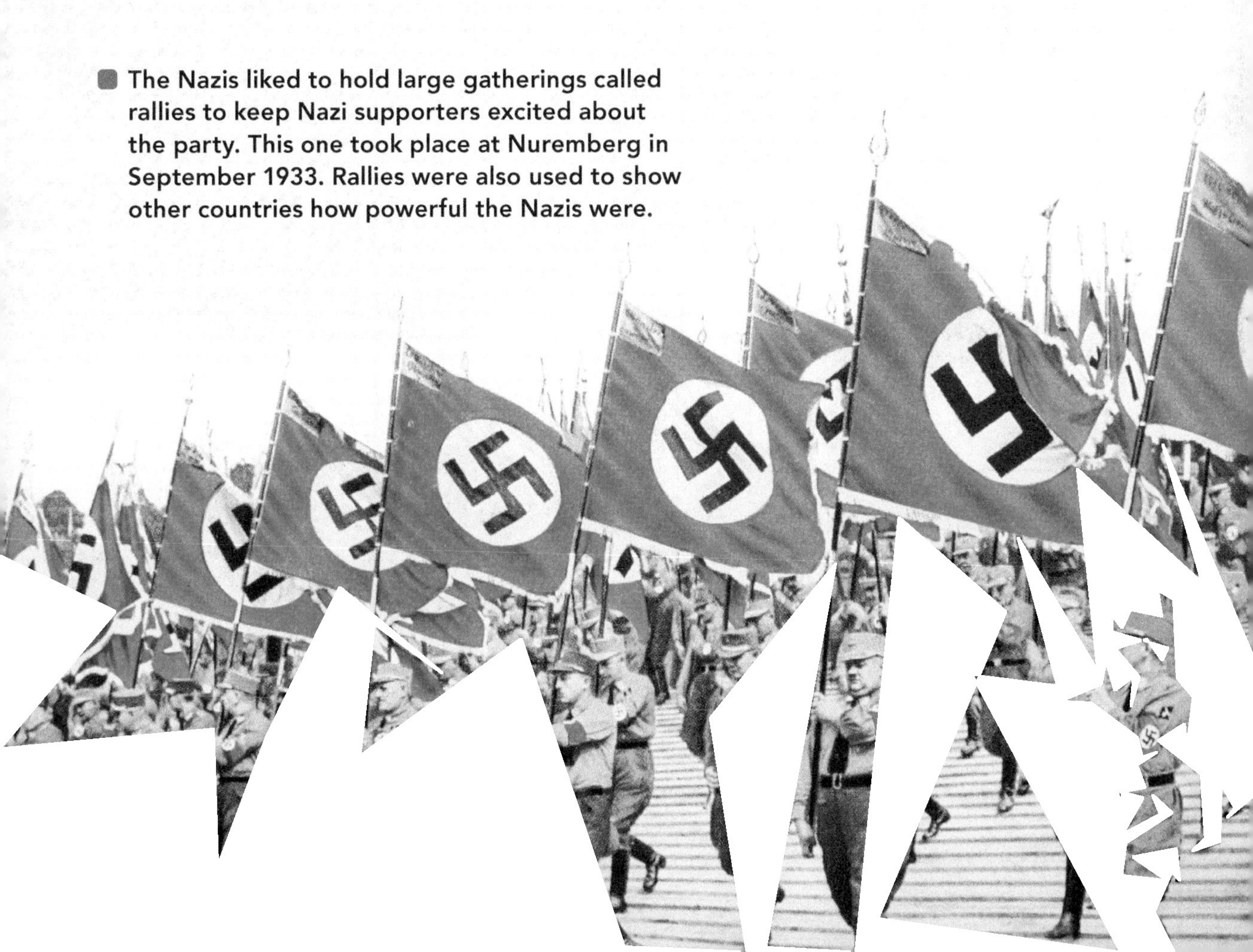

What Was Kristallnacht?

Some people think that the night of November 9–10, 1938 was the start of the Holocaust. It became known as Kristallnacht, which means Crystal Night. It is also called the Night of Broken Glass. Glass from the broken windows of Jewish businesses and homes covered the streets after the attacks.

On November 7, Ernst vom Rath was shot in France. Rath worked for the German government. Jewish teenager Herschel Grynszpan killed him. He was angry because Jewish people from Poland now living in Germany had been forced out by the Nazis. His parents were among those who had lost their homes and belongings.

Hitler went to Ernst vom Rath's funeral, which took place in Düsseldorf, Germany.

THE NOVEMBER POGROM

News about the shooting reached Germany on November 9. The Nazis did not need much of an excuse to attack Jewish people. They made it look as if it were unplanned. But the Nazis organized the violence. Attacks that are organized by the government or allowed to happen in this way are called **pogroms**.

Storm Troopers attacked Jewish shops, businesses, homes, and schools. Jewish places of worship were set on fire. Attacks happened across Germany and Austria that night. In some places, the violence continued through the next day. Sometimes, non-Jewish Germans joined in.

Kristallnacht led to the destruction of many Jewish places of worship, like this synagogue in Berlin.

HISTORY UNLOCKED

Fifteen-year-old Susanne von der Borch spoke to a few of the Hitler Youth leaders afterwards. "They said they had been at a shop … and they'd smashed the windows."

POLICE INSTRUCTIONS

Reinhard Heydrich was head of the German Security Police. He told the police that they were not to stop the attacks. Fire fighters should not put out fires. Heydrich ordered that Jewish businesses and homes could be "destroyed but not looted." Despite this order, many Jewish people afterwards claimed that their possessions had been taken. The police were told to arrest Jewish people, although only "healthy male Jews, not too old."

Attacks were made on 7,500 Jewish businesses. More than 1,000 synagogues were destroyed. At least 91 Jewish people were killed and 30,000 arrested.

THE CLEAN-UP

Afterwards, Jewish people were told that they were going to have to pay for the repairs and clean up the mess themselves. They were treated as if the rioting and attacks against them had been their fault.

NEW LAWS

After Kristallnacht, Jewish people had to face more new laws against them. Jewish children were no longer allowed to go to school after November 15. Curfews were then put in place. Curfews were rules that said Jewish people were not allowed to be outside their homes after 9 p.m. They were then banned from public places from December. Hermann Goering, a top Nazi official, was involved in making the new laws. He said, "I would not like to be a Jew in Germany." Those Jewish people who were able to do so left Germany. Those who remained faced a very difficult time.

The windows of this Jewish business were smashed during Kristallnacht.

What Happened After World War II Began?

On September 1, 1939, Germany **invaded** Poland. Britain and France declared war on Germany on September 3. This was the beginning of World War II. In the next year, Germany invaded other countries, including France, the Netherlands (Holland), and Belgium. Some Jewish people had escaped the Nazis before. Now they were under German control again.

Jewish people were rounded up by German soldiers in Warsaw in 1943.

POLAND

After the German invasion, limits on the freedom of Jewish people in Poland were set up. They were not even allowed to travel on a train without papers that proved they were free of **lice**. They had to get new papers every week.

GHETTOS

Jewish people were forced out of their own homes. They were sent to live in ghettos. Ghettos were usually set up in run-down areas. They were surrounded by walls or barbed wire. Police would guard the ghettos to keep Jewish people separate from other Germans.

People in the ghettos were given very little food. Often, there was no running water. Medical care was poor and this led to disease. Eight to ten people lived in one room on average. Between July and September 1942, 300,000 people from the Warsaw ghetto were killed in Treblinka death camp. The remaining Jewish people worked in German factories. They were allowed to continue working for the good of the Nazis.

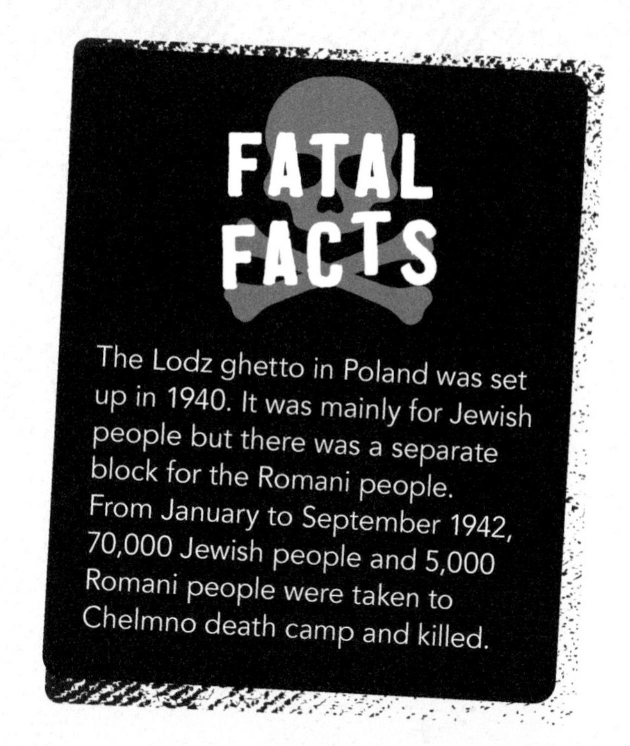

The Lodz ghetto in Poland was set up in 1940. It was mainly for Jewish people but there was a separate block for the Romani people. From January to September 1942, 70,000 Jewish people and 5,000 Romani people were taken to Chelmno death camp and killed.

This Warsaw ghetto building is now covered in pictures of Jewish people.

CONCENTRATION CAMPS

Concentration camps were places where people were forced to work for the Nazis. Prisoners included mainly Jewish people, but also gay people, Romani people, and prisoners of war. Anyone who spoke out against the Nazis was also imprisoned. The Nazis' plan was to work the prisoners to death. By 1939, there were six concentration camps. After the start of the war, the number increased because more people were imprisoned. Many of these were forced to be slave workers. Jobs included making weapons or sometimes building new camps.

This map shows the location of the death camps and some of the concentration camps in Germany and Poland.

Heinrich Himmler

Heinrich Himmler was born in Munich, Germany, in 1900. He was in charge of Hitler's bodyguards, the **SS**, and later all the police force. He gradually increased their numbers and their power. Himmler set up the first concentration camp at Dachau. He was later in charge of all camps.

Conditions in the camps were terrible. Bunk beds built for three people often housed many more. People had to sleep on their sides because there was so little room. There were no pillows or mattresses. There were too few toilets and sinks for the number of people in each block. People were given very little food, even when doing hard labor. Disease was common. Hundreds of thousands of people were worked to death.

Two prisoners at Buchenwald concentration camp are holding up the man in between them. If the guards thought he was too weak to work, he would be killed.

DISABLED PEOPLE

Starting in 1939, disabled children were killed by the Nazis. Parents did not know what was happening. They thought their children were going to receive better care.

After the war began, disabled adults were killed too. They were viewed as useless because they could not be put to work. To start with, people were killed by starvation or by a deadly injection. This took too long, though. Six centers were created to speed up the killing. People were now killed in large rooms that were filled with poisonous gas.

Hartheim Castle in Austria was one of the centers used to kill disabled people. It is thought that 250,000 were killed.

KILLING SQUADS

Germany invaded the **Soviet Union** in June 1941. Killing squads, called *Einsatzgruppen*, murdered Jewish people all over the Soviet Union. They would round up Jewish people and then shoot them.

Killing squads were used in the Soviet Union to murder large numbers of Jewish people.

The bodies would fall into big pits that had been dug already. In some places, such as Ukraine, local people would help. They could then choose what they wanted from what was on the bodies of the Jewish people who had been murdered.

In Kiev, Ukraine, 33,771 Jewish people were shot in just two days.

Adolf Eichmann

Adolf Eichmann was born in Solingen, Germany, in 1906. He became a member of the Nazi Party in the early 1930s. Eichmann was responsible for the mass **deportation** of Jews to death camps. After the war, he escaped to Argentina. Eichmann was finally arrested in 1960. He was put on trial in Jerusalem, Israel, and charged with the deportation, starvation, and murder of millions of Jewish people. Eichmann was found guilty and hanged in 1962.

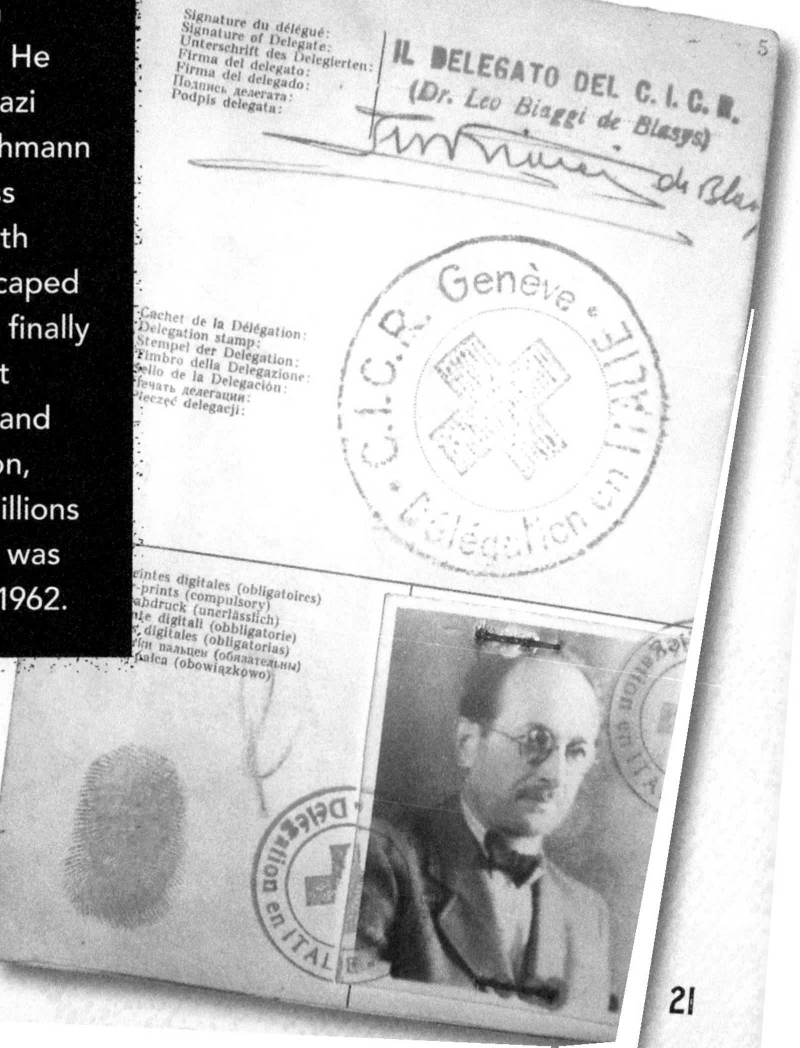
Signature du délégué:
Signature of Delegate:
Unterschrift des Delegierten:
Firma del delegato:
Firma del delegado:
Подпись делегата:
Podpis delegata:

IL DELEGATO DEL C.I.C.R.
(Dr. Leo Biaggi de Blasys)

5

Cachet de la Délégation:
Delegation stamp:
Stempel der Delegation:
Timbro della Delegazione:
Sello de la Delegación:
Печать делегации:
Pieczęć delegacji:

C.I.C.R. Genève • Délégation en ITALIE

...intes digitales (obligatoires)
...-prints (compulsory)
...abdruck (unerlässlich)
...te digitali (obbligatorie)
..., digitales (obligatorias)
...ки пальцев (обязательны)
...alca (obowiązkowo)

This is the Red Cross identity document that Adolf Eichmann used to enter Argentina.

What Was the Final Solution?

The Wannsee Conference took place on January 20, 1942. Reinhard Heydrich brought together leading Nazis to organize the Final Solution. This was an attempt to get rid of all Jewish people in Europe. Heydrich suggested that 11 million Jewish people would be killed. This was not just in areas controlled by Germany but also in countries such as Britain.

Hitler was not at Wannsee. It is thought that he agreed to the Final Solution at some point during 1941. But there were no written orders. On January 30, 1942, Hitler gave a speech in Berlin. He said that the result of the war would be total destruction of the Jewish people.

The Wannsee meeting was held at Wannsee House near Berlin, Germany.

GAS VANS

The *Einsatzgruppen* continued to kill Jewish people and **Communists** in the Soviet Union. But Heinrich Himmler was worried about the effect on his men of shooting so many people. He suggested using gas vans. These were being used in the Chelmno death camp. About 40 people were placed in a van. Gases from the van's exhaust pipe were pumped into the van. The people inside were killed.

At Treblinka death camp, prisoners were taken to a sealed room. The exhaust gases from vans were then pumped into the room. Other Jewish prisoners then removed the bodies and buried them.

Gas vans were used to kill more than 200,000 Polish Jewish people between December 1941 and spring 1943. Thousands of Romani and Soviet prisoners died in this way too.

Heinrich Himmler (left) and Reinhard Heydrich (center) were the men who organized the Final Solution.

DEATH CAMPS

Death camps were created to deliberately kill people. Six of them had been built in Poland by the end of 1941. Death camps such as Auschwitz II included gas chambers for killing the prisoners. After trying out different ways of killing, one was finally chosen. It was called Zyklon B. It was a chemical used to kill the lice on prisoners' clothes. If used in the air, it made a poisonous gas. Prisoners were told that they would be taking a shower. Instead of water, gas was pumped into the closed room. Many thousands could be killed at one time.

So many people were killed that huge piles of gas containers were formed.

Rudolf Höss was in charge of Auschwitz. At first, Auschwitz was a concentration and work camp. But then Auschwitz II was built by Russian prisoners in March 1942. It became the main center for killing people in Poland. At one end stood four gas chambers. These were capable of killing 12,000 people a day. Between 1.1 million and 1.5 million people, most of whom were Jewish, died at Auschwitz.

Rudolf Höss

Rudolf Höss fought in World War I. Like Hitler, he believed that Germany's loss was the fault of Jewish people. Starting off as a guard at Dachau, Höss rose through the ranks. Starting in May 1940, he ran Auschwitz. He lived nearby with his family. Höss liked people to think of him as an ordinary family man. He made sure that he never killed prisoners himself.

HISTORY UNLOCKED

When he was told about a new way of killing prisoners with gas, Höss was pleased. He said it, "had a calming effect on me. I always had a horror of the shootings."

After people were killed by gassing, the bodies were burned in the crematorium.

EXPERIMENTS

Josef Mengele was a doctor at Auschwitz starting in May 1943. He carried out experiments on prisoners. These were not ordinary scientific experiments. They were very cruel. One of them involved leaving prisoners outside with no clothes in freezing temperatures. Mengele did not care about the prisoners at all. One story tells of one of the women's blocks being full of lice. He ordered that the 750 women living there be gassed. Then the block could be cleared of lice.

Josef Mengele (second from left) showed no guilt about the experiments he carried out on prisoners.

AUSCHWITZ III

Auschwitz III was built by IG Farben, a chemical business. They forced prisoners to work for them. Prisoners were worked hard. Out of nearly 40,000 prisoners, over 25,000 died.

HISTORY UNLOCKED

Nazi Joseph Goebbels kept a diary. On March 27, 1942, he wrote about plans for Jewish people.

"Not much will remain of the Jews. On the whole it can be said that about 60 percent of them will have to be liquidated [killed], whereas only 40 percent can be used for forced labor."

HUNGARY

In March 1944, the Nazis invaded Hungary. They knew that the Soviet army was getting closer. But they wanted to get rid of all the Jewish people in Hungary. Adolf Eichmann went there himself. He organized the deportation of over 434,000 Jewish people in eight weeks. Many were murdered as soon as they arrived at Auschwitz.

As soon as people arrived at Auschwitz, they were sorted into groups: death or work. Women with children were sent straight to their deaths.

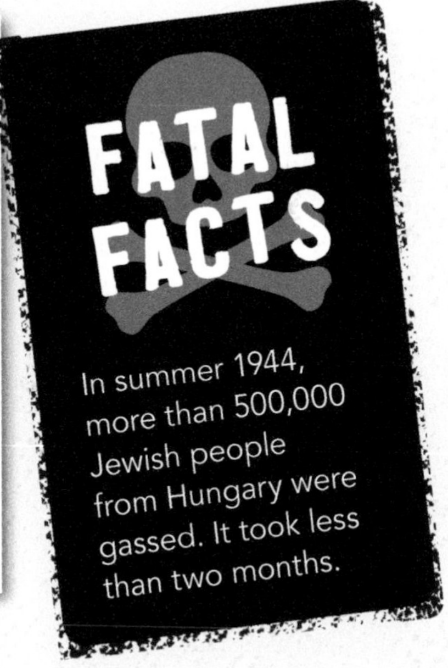

FATAL FACTS

In summer 1944, more than 500,000 Jewish people from Hungary were gassed. It took less than two months.

What Did Non-Jewish People Know?

In the early 1930s, both non-Jewish and Jewish Germans lived together peacefully. After the Nazis came to power in 1933, their feelings about Jewish people gradually spread to non-Jewish citizens. By 1939, people were no longer speaking out against anti-Semitism. For some, this was a result of fear. They were too scared to go against the Nazis. They knew that it might mean imprisonment or death if they were caught helping Jewish people.

Some people eventually joined in with the cruel treatment of Jewish people. Others did not take part but had some idea at least of what was happening. And there were those who decided to help the Jewish people as much as they could.

Raoul Wallenberg was a businessman and government official who helped to save thousands of Jewish people in Hungary.

During the war, people may not have known how many Jewish people were already in concentration camps, but they knew that they were being rounded up. Hannelore Mahler was a Jewish woman from the city of Krefeld, Germany. In September 1944, Jewish people were rounded up and marched in front of a church as people were leaving. "They had to have seen us," she said.

Non-Jewish people had heard so much about how terrible the Jewish people were that many of them believed it. Walter Sanders was a communications officer on the Russian front. "When the Jews were deported, we knew that something was going to happen to them." He told family and friends the awful things he had seen when he came home on leave.

The Nazis tried to keep what they were doing as secret as possible. Above the gates of Auschwitz were the words "Work sets you free." This was a cruel sign. Prisoners in the camps were starved and killed there.

What Help Did the Jewish People Get?

From 1933 to 1939, 70,000 **refugees** went to Britain. This included 10,000 children—mainly Jewish children from Austria and Germany—who arrived on trains as part of the Kindertransport program.

Children from Germany traveled on the first Kindertransport to Britain in December 1938.

The United States allowed a fixed number of people into the country each year. In November 1938, President Franklin D Roosevelt refused to increase that number. But European Jews already in the United States were allowed to stay. Others entered gradually over the next few years.

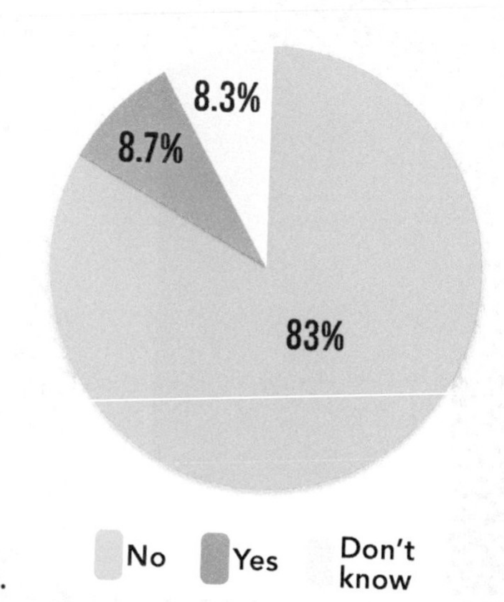

In early 1939, Americans were asked if they would allow more Jewish people into the country if they could. This pie chart shows the result. Of the 8.7 percent in favor, nearly 70 percent were Jewish.

In Poland, the Polish people had been badly treated by the Nazis. But some still handed over their Jewish neighbors. Even Jewish groups in other countries did not show support. The Catholic Church did not help either, although some Catholic individuals did.

This statue of the children who journeyed on the Kindertransport is in Gdańsk, Poland.

LATER IN THE WAR

Four prisoners escaped from Auschwitz in 1944. Their stories made it clear what was happening in the camps. Many people have asked why nothing was done by the **Allies** at this point. Jewish people from Hungary wrote to Allied leaders asking them to bomb the railroad lines leading to Auschwitz. But this did not happen. Britain and the United States could have taken in more refugees. But this did not happen. Some people think it was because Allied leaders were also anti-Semitic. Others think defeating the Nazis was more of a priority.

RISKING LIVES TO HELP

But some people did their best to help. They often did so with great risk to their own lives. They knew that if they were caught, they would be imprisoned themselves. Henry Singer's sister survived because she was hidden by a German family. Blanche Benedick was a Jewish girl from Denmark. Her family was helped by the family of her best friend, Mona. They were not Jewish. Blanche's family were hidden in a fishing boat and taken to Sweden. They survived. In October 1943, there were about 8,000 Jewish people in Copenhagen, Denmark. Only 450 were caught by the Nazis.

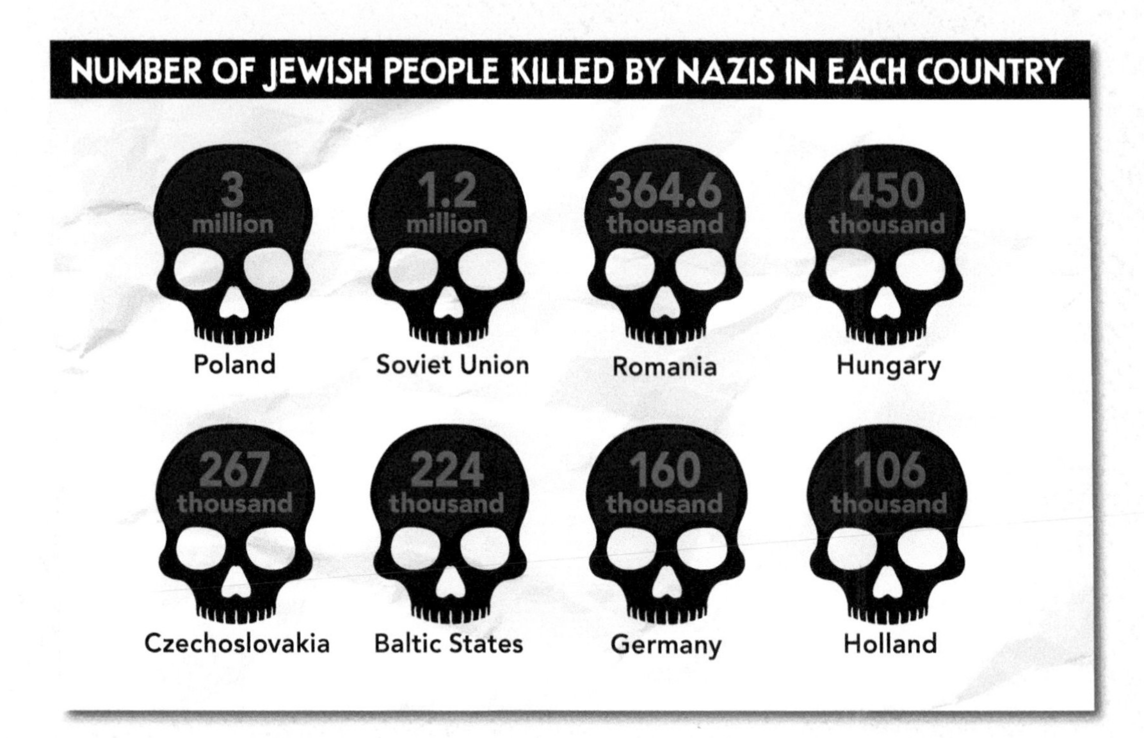

THE WARSAW GHETTO UPRISING

Jewish people did everything they could to help themselves. The Warsaw Ghetto Uprising took place in April and May 1943. It was discovered that everyone was to be moved out of the ghetto. This meant that everyone would be killed. A group within the ghetto called the Jewish Fighting Organization (ZOB) was formed. They decided to fight back.

There were about 750 Jewish people involved in the fighting. ZOB had very few weapons, but they did injure and kill some Nazis. They held out for four weeks, but the ghetto was eventually destroyed. Some Jewish people were gassed and others were sent to death camps. The Uprising helped to encourage others to fight back.

On May 8, the Germans found the bunker containing ZOB's leaders. Many of ZOB's fighters took their own lives, including Mordechai Anielewicz, ZOB's commander.

People were forced out of the underground bunkers by German soldiers at the end of the Warsaw Ghetto Uprising.

ANNE FRANK

Anne Frank was born in Frankfurt, Germany, in 1929. After Hitler came to power in 1933, life for Jewish people became more and more difficult. Anne's family moved to Amsterdam in the Netherlands. In May 1940, the Nazis invaded the Netherlands.

The laws against Jewish people in Germany were now enforced in the Netherlands. On July 5, 1942, Anne's sister, Margot, received a letter. It said she was to be sent to work in Germany. Everyone knew that this probably meant death. The Franks went into hiding, along with four other Jewish people. They stayed in a secret annex at the back of Anne's father's office building. Non-Jewish office workers, including Miep Gies, helped them to survive.

Anne Frank was given a diary for her 13th birthday. This is a page from the diary.

For two years, the Franks lived in very cramped conditions. They couldn't go outside or make much noise. But Anne knew that things could be worse. In May 1943, she wrote:

"If I just think of how we live here, I usually come to the conclusion that it is a paradise compared with how other Jews who are not in hiding must be living."

When writing in her diary, Anne pretended to write to a friend called Kitty.

ARRESTED

Eventually, the Franks were found. On August 4, 1944, they were arrested and sent to Westerbork concentration camp. In November 1944, Anne and Margot were sent to Bergen-Belsen. There, Anne died of typhus in March 1945.

Anne wrote a diary while hiding from the Nazis. Miep Gies found and kept the diary after the Franks were taken to Westerbork. After the war, Anne's father published it. He did so because Anne had always wanted to be an author.

What Happened to Survivors?

Toward the end of the war, SS guards sent nearly 60,000 prisoners on a death march from Auschwitz, Poland, to Germany. Many prisoners had been killed before the march and up to 15,000 died on the way. Some starved or froze to death. Some were shot. The Nazis did not want any prisoners being caught alive. The Nazis had blown up areas of Auschwitz where the bodies were burned. They did not want people finding out how bad things had been.

While most of the remaining Auschwitz prisoners had been moved by the SS, the Soviet army found 7,000 people left there in January 1945. They found other things too. There were human teeth and hair, and many thousands of sets of children's clothes.

HISTORY UNLOCKED

Lilly Appelbaum Malnik describes the death march from Auschwitz to Bergen-Belsen.

"And we started walking, we walked for days. ... We heard gun shots and they were shooting people in the back who couldn't keep up with the walking."

These were some of the things found at Auschwitz.

BUCHENWALD

Orders had come from the Gestapo, the Nazi secret police, to blow up Buchenwald concentration camp, including the prisoners. But most of the SS guards had fled when they heard the Allies were close. They had still managed to send 28,000 on a death march from the camp, though. One in three died on the march. The guards had also emptied water tanks before they left. In February 1945, there had been 112,000 prisoners at Buchenwald. When the U.S. army arrived on April 11, 1945, 21,000 remained. They were still suffering and dying. They had little food and no water.

U.S. soldiers (far left) take children to the hospital after they were rescued from Buchenwald.

BERGEN-BELSEN

The British army freed nearly 60,000 prisoners from Bergen-Belsen concentration camp in April 1945. The soldiers were not prepared for the shock of all the dead bodies. About 10,000 bodies had not been buried. They had been left in piles around the camp.

HISTORY UNLOCKED

Teenager Edith Birkin was at Bergen-Belsen when the British Army arrived.

"Most of us couldn't go to greet them, because we were so weak and tired. ... We were always imagining that when we are liberated [freed] we are going to be dancing, and kissing them—and I don't think they wanted to be kissed by us to be honest! ... we didn't think we were so dreadful you know, but to them we looked absolutely awful of course."

British soldiers provided food for the freed Bergen-Belsen prisoners.

Most of the people in the camp were very ill. Josef Kramer had run the camp. He had decided that the best way to deal with the illness was not to feed the prisoners. In March, over 18,000 prisoners, including Anne Frank, died. If people were not ill, they were very weak. Some were so weak that their bodies could not take in the food the British soldiers had brought. They died.

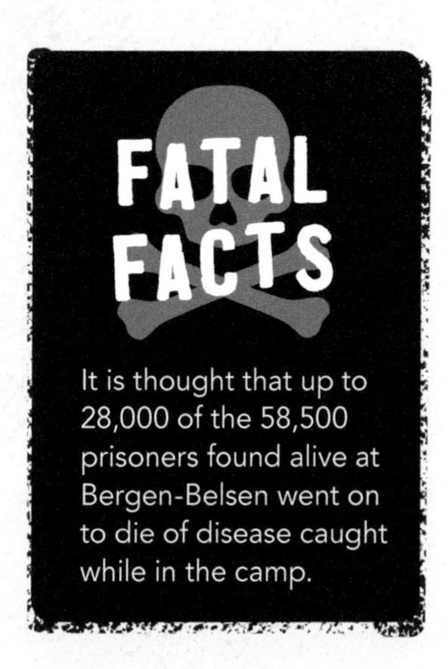

It is thought that up to 28,000 of the 58,500 prisoners found alive at Bergen-Belsen went on to die of disease caught while in the camp.

A gravestone for Anne Frank and her sister has been placed at Bergen-Belsen.

OTHER CAMPS

The story at other camps was similar. Soldiers found that camps had been very overcrowded. They found that hygiene was poor. They found that many prisoners were barely alive.

Nobody knows exactly how many civilians, or non-soldiers, were killed by the Nazis. The numbers shown in this graph are based on the best guesses of experts.

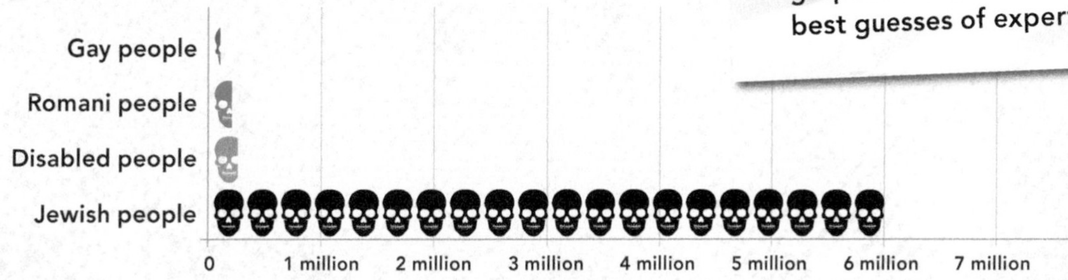

What Effect Did the Holocaust Have?

The horror of what happened during the Holocaust slowly came to light. As prisoners from the camps were freed, soldiers and reporters told of what they had seen. Most people were shocked. The Allies began to argue about how to deal with the Nazis and where Jewish survivors would go. Would the people who had lost so much—family, homes, belongings—be given help to live?

WHERE WOULD JEWISH SURVIVORS GO?

Many Jewish people who survived the Holocaust had nowhere to go. Few countries were willing to take many people. By 1947, about 300,000 Jewish people were still homeless.

Anti-Semitism did not disappear either. In July 1946, at least 42 Jewish people were killed at Kielce, Poland. Forty were injured. It was a way of telling Holocaust survivors not to return to Poland. Over 75,000 Jewish people left the country in the three months after this attack.

CREATING ISRAEL

Palestine was under British control. Mainly Arabs lived there alongside a small number of Jewish people. The United States suggested the Jewish people live in Palestine. At first Britain disagreed. Then in 1947 they decided to hand over control of Palestine to the **United Nations**. It was decided that Arabs and Jewish people should share Palestine. Arabs were unhappy about having to give up their land to create space for Jewish people. But in May 1948, the State of Israel was set up for Jewish people. Decades of war and unrest have followed.

Jewish children arrive by boat in Tel Aviv, Israel, in April 1946.

JUSTICE

The Allies had different ideas about how to get **justice** for the millions who had died. The British had suggested killing the leaders whenever they were caught. The United States and Russia wanted the men to be tried in a court of law. The problem was that no country had ever tried the leaders of another country in this way.

THE NUREMBERG TRIALS

Eventually, in October 1945, the Nuremberg trials began. Twenty-two Nazis, including some of the Nazi leaders, were to be judged for crimes against peace and humanity, and for war crimes. War crimes are actions carried out during war that go against the acceptable rules of war. The killing of Jewish people in the camps is an example. Some Nazis were put to death as a result of the trials, while others went to prison.

MAKING AMENDS

After 1953, the German government paid money to Jewish Holocaust survivors. The money was to try to apologize for what happened. Other European countries, such as France, have paid too.

A Holocaust monument in Berlin, Germany, has 2,711 concrete blocks.

GENOCIDE

The word **genocide** was created in 1943 by a Polish-Jewish lawyer called Raphael Lemkin. He wanted to put a name to what the Nazis were doing. Lemkin wanted genocide to be an international crime. The United Nations agreed. Genocide was defined as deliberately aiming to destroy, either completely or partly, a national, racial, or religious group.

After the horrors of the Holocaust, it would be easy to think that nothing like that would ever happen again. But it has. In the late 1970s, two million people were killed in Cambodia. In 1994, thousands died in Rwanda because of their race. The mass killings of Bosnian Muslims by the Serbs in 1995 is another example.

REMEMBERING THE HOLOCAUST

International Holocaust Remembrance Day is marked on January 27. Jewish people all over the world celebrate their survival and remember those who died. It reminds us that we need to understand that everyone is different and we should embrace those differences.

This monument to the Holocaust is at Dachau concentration camp in Germany.

Timeline

1921

July Hitler takes over leadership of the National Socialist German Workers' Party.

1933

January The Nazi Party takes power in Germany; Hitler is made Chancellor.

March 20 Dachau, the first Nazi concentration camp, opens.

April 1 Hitler demands that Jewish shops and businesses are boycotted.

1935

September 15 The Nuremberg laws limit the freedom of Jewish people in Germany.

1938

November 9–10 Jewish people, Jewish buildings and places of worship are attacked during Kristallnacht.

1939

September Germany invades Poland; Britain and France declare war on Germany.

1941

June 22 Germany invades the Soviet Union.

June *Einsatzgruppen* begin killing Jewish people in the Soviet Union.

1942

January 20 The Final Solution is discussed at the Wannsee Conference.

1943

April 19 The Warsaw Ghetto Uprising takes place.

1945

January 18 Nearly 60,000 prisoners leave on a death march from Auschwitz.

January 27 The Soviet army frees prisoners from Auschwitz.

April 11 The U.S. army frees prisoners from Buchenwald.

April 15 The British army frees prisoners from Bergen-Belsen.

October The Nuremberg trials begin.

1948

May 14 The State of Israel is created.

GLOSSARY

Allies (AL-eyz)—countries that fought against Germany in World War II

anti-Semitism (an-ti SEM-i-ti-zem)—strong feelings of hatred against Jewish people for no clear reason

Aryan (AIR-ee-un)—white northern European person considered by Nazis to be better than any other race

citizen (SI-tuh-zuhn)—member of a country or state who has the right to live there

communist (KAHM-yuh-nist)—person who believes in communism, a way of organizing a country so that all the land, houses, and factories belong to the government, and the profits are shared by all

concentration camp (kahn-suhn-TRAY-shuhn KAMP)—place in which people are imprisoned

death camp (DETH KAMP)—place where people were sent to be killed

deport (di-PORT)—remove people from their homes and send to a concentration or death camp

gas chamber (GASS CHAYM-buhr)—room that was filled with gas in order to kill people inside

genocide (JEN-oh-side)—organized killing of an entire cultural or political group

ghetto (GET-oh)—area in a town or city where certain groups of people, such as Jewish people, were sent to live after being removed from their own homes

invade (in-VADE)—send armed forces into another country in order to take it over

Jewish people (JOO-ish PEE-pul)—people who follow the religion or culture of Judaism

justice (JUHSS-tiss)—when punishment is given for breaking the law

lice (LYSE)—bloodsucking insects that live on humans and other mammals

pogrom (POH-gruhm)—government-organized murder

political party (puh-LIT-uh-kuhl PAR-tee)—group of people who share the same beliefs about how the government should work

refugee (ref-yuh-JEE)—person who has been forced to leave his or her home to escape war or persecution

rights (RITES)—things that everyone has a right to such as the right to freedom and to not be treated unfairly

Soviet Union (SOH-vee-et YOON-yuhn)—former group of 15 republics that included Russia, Ukraine, and other nations in eastern Europe and northern Asia

SS (ess-ess)—men who were originally Hitler's bodyguards and who later ran the camps

Storm Troopers (STORM TROOP-ers)—mainly former soldiers who were responsible for violent attacks on Jewish people and others

United Nations (yoo-NI-ted NAY-shuns)—international organization that encourages peace and cooperation between countries

READ MORE

Carlson Berne, Emma. *Escaping the Nazis on the Kindertransport*. Mankato, Minn.: Capstone Press, 2017.

Down, Susan Brophy. *Irena Sendler*. St Catharines, ONT, Canada: Crabtree Publishing, 2012.

Freeburg, Jessica. *Fight for Survival: The Story of the Holocaust*. Mankato, Minn.: Capstone Press, 2015.

Herman, Gail. *What Was the Holocaust?*. New York: Grosset and Dunlap, 2017.

Roy, Jennifer. *Jars of Hope: How One Woman Helped Save 2,500 Children During the Holocaust*. Mankato, Minn.: Capstone Press, 2015.

Thomson, Ruth. *Terezin: Voices from the Holocaust*. Somerville, Mass.: Candlewick Press, 2013.

Zapruder, Alexandra. *Anne Frank*. Washington D.C.: National Geographic Society, 2013.

Internet Sites

FactHound offers a safe, fun way to find Internet sites related to this book. All of the sites on FactHound have been researched by our staff.

Here's all you do:

Visit *www.facthound.com*

Type in this code: 9781484641668

Critical Thinking Questions

Which parts of this book did you find the most interesting? What subjects would you like to know more about?

Investigate the history of Judaism, the Jewish religion. Look at Islam, Christianity, and Judaism and find the ways they are similar and the ways they are different.

Research more about the people who helped Jewish people during the Holocaust, such as Oskar Schindler, Irena Sendler, and Nicholas Winton.

See if you can find out about anti-Jewish pogroms, such as those that took place at the time of the Crusades.

INDEX